P9-DNC-817

Illustrations copyright © 1992 by Dorothée Duntze
All rights reserved. No part of this book may be reproduced or utilized in any form
or by any means, electronic or mechanical, including photocopying,
recording or by any information storage and retrieval system
without permission in writing from the publisher.

Published in the United States by North-South Books Inc., New York.

Published simultaneously in Great Britain,
Canada, Australia and New Zealand by North-South Books,
an imprint of Nord-Süd Verlag AG, Gossau Zürich, Switzerland.

Library of Congress Cataloging-in-Publication Data
Twelve days of Christmas (English folk song)
The twelve days of Christmas / illustrated by Dorothée Duntze.
Summary: On each of the twelve days of Christmas,
more and more gifts arrive from the recipient's true love.
1. Folk songs, English—England—Texts. 2. Christmas music.
[1. Folk songs—England. 2. Christmas music.]
I. Duntze, Dorothée, ill. II. Title.
PZ8.3.T8517 1992
782.42'1723'0268–dc20 91-32359
ISBN 1-55858-151-0 (Trade binding)
ISBN 1-55858-152-9 (Library binding)

British Library Cataloguing in Publication Data
Duntze, Dorothée
Twelve Days of Christmas
I. Title
782.28 [J]
ISBN 1-55858-151-0

1 3 5 7 9 10 8 6 4 2
Printed in Belgium

The Twelve Days of Christmas

ILLUSTRATED BY Dorothée Duntze

WITHDRAWN
Irvington Public Library
Irvington-on-Hudson, N. Y.

North-South Books / NEW YORK

On the first day of Christmas
My true love sent to me
A partridge in a pear tree.

On the second day of Christmas
My true love sent to me
Two turtle doves,
And a partridge in a pear tree.

On the third day of Christmas
My true love sent to me
Three French hens,
Two turtle doves,
And a partridge in a pear tree.

On the fourth day of Christmas
My true love sent to me
Four calling birds,
Three French hens,
Two turtle doves,
And a partridge in a pear tree.

On the fifth day of Christmas
My true love sent to me
Five gold rings,
Four calling birds,
Three French hens,
Two turtle doves,
And a partridge in a pear tree.

On the sixth day of Christmas
My true love sent to me
Six geese a-laying,
Five gold rings,
Four calling birds,
Three French hens,
Two turtle doves,
And a partridge in a pear tree.

On the seventh day of Christmas
My true love sent to me
Seven swans a-swimming,
Six geese a-laying,
Five gold rings,
Four calling birds,
Three French hens,
Two turtle doves,
And a partridge in a pear tree.

On the eighth day of Christmas
My true love sent to me
Eight maids a-milking,
Seven swans a-swimming,
Six geese a-laying,
Five gold rings,
Four calling birds,
Three French hens,
Two turtle doves,
And a partridge in a pear tree.

On the ninth day of Christmas
My true love sent to me
Nine drummers drumming,
Eight maids a-milking,
Seven swans a-swimming,
Six geese a-laying,

Five gold rings,
Four calling birds,
Three French hens,
Two turtle doves,
And a partridge in a pear tree.

On the tenth day of Christmas
My true love sent to me
Ten pipers piping,
Nine drummers drumming,
Eight maids a-milking,
Seven swans a-swimming,
Six geese a-laying,
Five gold rings,
Four calling birds,
Three French hens,
Two turtle doves,
And a partridge in a pear tree.

On the eleventh day of Christmas
My true love sent to me
Eleven ladies dancing,
Ten pipers piping,
Nine drummers drumming,
Eight maids a-milking,
Seven swans a-swimming,

Six geese a-laying,
Five gold rings,
Four calling birds,
Three French hens,
Two turtle doves,
And a partridge in a pear tree.

On the twelfth day of Christmas
My true love sent to me

Twelve lords a-leaping,

Eleven ladies dancing,

Ten pipers piping,

Nine drummers drumming,

Eight maids a-milking,

Seven swans a-swimming,

Six geese a-laying,

Five gold rings,

Four calling birds,

Three French hens,

Two turtle doves,

And a partridge in a pear tree.

IRVINGTON PUBLIC LIBRARY

3 1012 13025 6475